Radical Inclusivity
Expanding Our Minds Beyond
Dualistic Thinking

JEFF CARREIRA

Radical Inclusivity:
Expanding our Minds Beyond Dualistic Thinking
By Jeff Carreira

Copyright © 2014
Emergence Education & Jeff Carreira

ISBN: 978-0615964911
ISBN-13: 0615964915

Emergence Education
230 Stampers Street
Philadelphia, PA 01947

Cover Photography by Doug Ciarelli
Cover Design by www.choosefreeagency.com

The Philosophy Is Not a Luxury Book Series
Dedicated to the profound utility of questioning reality

Our busy and at times overwhelming lives tempt us to see philosophy as a luxury item that we cannot afford.

It's not.

In fact, in the face of life's inevitable challenges, philosophy, which is the pursuit of truth, is essential.

What we believe or assume to be true dictates how we act, and how we act creates how the world is. This is a simple, unalterable, and somewhat unforgiving fact.

If we want to create a better world, then one of the most important things we can do is inquire into the nature of our beliefs and assumptions about what is real and true.

This book series was established to publish books that will inspire us into new realms of discovery.

CONTENTS

INTRODUCTION

I believe that we stand in much the same relation to the whole of the universe as our canine and feline pets do to the whole of human life. They inhabit our drawing rooms and libraries. They take part in scenes of whose significance they have no inkling. They are merely tangent to curves of history the beginnings and ends and forms of which pass wholly beyond their ken. So we are tangents to the wider life of things.   William James

This book is an invitation to a level of philosophical inquiry that you might not know exists.

Our journey begins with a description of some of my experiences of profound states of consciousness and the ways I have come to understand them. We go on to discuss how such dramatic shifts occur and how they can be catalyzed. We conclude by exploring the significance of experiences like these in terms of a larger shift in consciousness that many of us seem to be in the midst of.

You will notice that the writing style used is personal, fluid, fast moving, and at times poetic. That is because I want to avoid giving the impression that a new consciousness can be captured in words. What I am sharing is not knowledge or information. It is not meant to explain how you should think. My intention is to use my experience to initiate an inquiry that will inspire you to think about your own experience and open up some questions worth thinking about.

CHAPTER ONE

THE EXPERIENCE OF RADICAL INCLUSIVITY

Jeff Carreira

The first time I was engulfed by the realization of Radical Inclusivity was during a sixty-day meditation retreat under the guidance of my spiritual teacher. As I sat from morning until evening following the simple instruction "Let everything be as it is," I found myself transported to an experience of consciousness that I had no way to anticipate.

Sitting hour after hour with my legs crossed I made supreme effort to follow those simple instructions. I simply allowed whatever I was experiencing to be exactly as it was without making any effort at all to do anything. The goal was to truly do nothing and resist the temptation to engage in any way with any part of my experience.

It is a practice of perfect passivity—literally asking me to do nothing at all.

As the hours of meditation became days of meditation, I saw over and over again how I would catch myself in the earnest effort of trying to do nothing. Every time I would catch myself I would realize that "trying to do nothing" is still doing something—and doing something is not doing nothing. So with each realization I would stop doing something and start doing nothing.

After relentless hours spent revolving through this cycle of entrapment and escape, I began to realize that every time I "stopped doing something" I was doing something. Stopping doing something was still doing *something,* and the goal was to do nothing. If stopping doing something was still not doing nothing, then how could I do nothing? I spent prolonged periods locked in the mental gymnastics of trying to do nothing, while realizing over and over again that trying to do nothing was still doing something. It was supremely frustrating, like trying to look at the back of your eyeballs. It seemed that the spiritual physics would not allow me to do nothing.

Eventually I realized something that was so obvious that I couldn't see it before. If the instruction is to let everything be as it is, I literally couldn't fail. Absolutely everything that happens is already the way it is, and there is no reason to do anything about it. Whenever I realized that I had spent the last twenty minutes locked in an imaginary struggle to let everything be as it is—then that is the way it was. In the moment of realizing it there was nothing to do except see what happens next. Anything that you experience and anything that you do will always be the way it is. Meditation is not different from just being—it is a practice of perfect acceptance.

Once I realized this, my experience of meditation changed completely even though nothing was different. I was still struggling in all the same ways. I was still having breakthrough experiences of bliss and illumination, still living through prolonged, tormenting bouts of doubt and frustration. Nothing was different except it all stopped bothering me.

It was so obvious. The instruction is to allow everything be the way it is, and the way it is is already the way it is. Sometimes we are sitting quietly aware; at other times we get lost in thought and struggle; and other times we wake up from being lost in thought. That is the cycle of consciousness that we experience all the time. That is the way it is.

The realization of Radical Inclusivity in the context of this meditation practice is the realization that no matter what I experience, it is the way it is, and there is nothing I could do to make it otherwise. No matter what appears to be happening, everything will always already be the way it is, including thinking that it is not. At this point in my meditation practice something finished. I stopped feeling like there was anything I could do. I stopped wanting anything to be different from the way that it already was. Everything was different, and nothing had changed.

In meditation you stop needing to do anything when you accept that everything is already included in the instruction of letting everything be as it is. That is the realization of Radical Inclusiveness. It is the recognition, in one context or another, that everything is already included in some larger whole— that the perception that there was ever anything outside that needed to be included was always an illusion.

It will take some explanation and examples to make this idea clear. In this book, as we go through different examples of how Radical Inclusivity shows up in different contexts, we will see that it is always some form of recognition that everything is already included.

Going back for a moment to my experience on retreat, from this point on my experience was one of unbroken trust in the fact of Radical Inclusivity. The cascade of insight and realization was now free to move through me because I had stopped doing anything to distract myself. There was no reason to do anything but sit still, pay attention, and relax. Everything else was just the way that it was and always would be. In that deep state of calm abidance I experienced profound spiritual openings and energetic breakthroughs.

My first encounters with Radical Inclusivity came as realizations during meditation practice, but over time I have come to realize that the fact of Radical Inclusivity goes far beyond the experience of deep meditation. Inclusivity is an inescapable and all-pervasive property of reality. It is the recognition that everything is already part of a larger whole. Everything is already inside of something else, and ultimately there is no outside at all.

Inclusivity does not become radical until it becomes infinite. My experience of inclusivity during a meditation retreat did not become radical until I realized that any experience I ever had, or could ever have, was already exactly the way it was and could not be otherwise. Following the meditation instruction "Let everything be as it is" meant that there was no way to not be meditating. Everything already is as it is, regardless of what I do.

The realization of Radical Inclusivity is the recognition that you are already on the inside (although what *inside* means may be different in different circumstances and contexts.) Ultimately there is no way out because there is no outside that is not inside. The experience of Radical Inclusivity points to the indisputable fact that there is no outside to reality.

My experience lead me to an extraordinary and paradoxical realization. There is a part of me that is always aware even if I am not aware of it. Consciousness, I discovered, is radically inclusive. Everything exists inside of consciousness. In the third chapter I will return to this notion to explore it in detail, but for now you will have to take my word for it when I say that there is a part of me that is always awake even if I am not aware of it.

Let's take a moment to examine the weirdness[1] of a realization like this. There is a part of me that is always aware even if I am not aware of it. The paradox here is that I seem to be aware and not aware at the same time; or that there are in fact two of me, one that is always aware and one that is sometimes not aware of that.

It seems that the experience of Radical Inclusivity will always—at least for the foreseeable future—include some level of paradox because these experiences actually exist in a different level of consciousness. Our minds are currently running in an operating system that we could call dualistic thinking,[2] which distinguishes things in terms of pairs of

[1] I borrow the word *weirdness* from Timothy Morton and Graham Harman, who are pioneering the philosophy of speculative realism. They both believe that embracing weirdness is essential for us to begin to see ourselves through to a new vision of reality.

[2] I recently spoke about "dualistic thinking" with Bonnitta Roy, founder of the Magellan Courses. Roy is working to determine an alternative way of thinking that she calls onto-logics.

opposites—this/that, here/there, now/then, inside/outside, etc.

Our experiences of Radical Inclusivity are paradoxical in nature because they actually exist in a new level of consciousness. When we are in the middle of them, they don't feel paradoxical at all. They seem normal and as obvious as the back of your hand. Later, when we return to our normal level of consciousness and think back about the experience of Radical Inclusivity, it *becomes* paradoxical. That is because what had seemed normal and obvious when we were experiencing it in one state of consciousness now looks impossible from the vantage point of another.

These jumps in consciousness resemble the hyperspace jumps I loved in science fiction stories as a child. You start out in one spot in the universe and then hit the hyperdrive, and, boom, you are on the other side of the universe. In even more exciting variations of the theme you actually end up in a new universe, one that occupies a space and time different from the universe you came from.

The metaphor of hyperspace is a good one to help us understand how we come to experience Radical Inclusivity. These experiences of the infinite inside of reality happen in a different universe or, if you will, a different dimension of reality.

One characteristic of this kind of travel is that it happens spontaneously, without any elapsing of time or traversing of space. You were in one place, and then you were in another. And the new place you end up in, especially if it is not just a different location in your universe but a different universe altogether, can be very weird.[3]

The structure of matter and the laws of time, space, and causality might all be completely different. There is simply no way to know what you will find in a new universe and no way to be sure that your mind, conditioned by the reality of one universe, will be useful at all in understanding anything in the new one. This can make things very weird.

Our trips into the new universe of Radical Inclusivity are similar. They exist in a different reality, a different consciousness from the one that our minds have been trained in. We travel into these experiences instantaneously and spontaneously with no time elapsing and no space being traversed. We are simply in one consciousness and then find ourselves in another. The return trip, assuming we make one, is the same. You were there, and now you are here. Sometimes the shift back is so subtle that we don't realize we have returned until the next time we are there.

Of course every way that I attempt to describe Radical Inclusivity in writing will be subject to the problem that I have to do it with the language of our current level of consciousness. That means I cannot ultimately capture it. The Romantic writers of the late eighteenth century were among the first to become aware of the problem of describing other dimensions of consciousness in words. Many of them used opium as their hyperdrive into new realms of being. Thomas de Quincey, for instance, spent Saturday nights with an opium-soaked rag in his pocket that he would suck on before entering an opera, concert, or play so that

---

[3] Edwin Abbott's 1884 novel *Flatland* still gives one of the most accessible and profound explications of inter-dimensional travel.

he could watch from the vantage point of an alternate consciousness. When trying to capture alternative consciousness in words, they chose poetry as their medium. Poetry allows for enough ambiguity of meaning to allow it to become a launch pad beyond the consciousness inherent in the language being used. Some Romantics even believed that only the abstract nature of music made a viable medium for chronicling journeys into consciousness.

I have also learned that when trying to describe the ineffable the liberal use of metaphor and analogy is required. These nonliteral means of communication allow us to point to new realms of consciousness while avoiding getting stuck in literal interpretation.

Radical Inclusivity can be thought of as an experience of nondual consciousness that occurs when the duality between inside and outside collapses. It is a hyperdrive that can take us from this universe to another. It happens instantaneously with no time having elapsed and no space being traversed.

In this book I will be describing a practice that I call the Art of Staying on the Inside, which gives us access to the experience of Radical Inclusivity and the new realm of consciousness that it occurs within.

One last thing that I want to state again at the start of this book is that one can recognize Radical Inclusivity in many different contexts. Meditation happened to be the context of my first encounter with it, but I don't want to limit the experience to that practice. Instead, I intend to show that meditation is only one form of the Art of Staying on the Inside and go on to present others.

Many of the philosophers and thinkers that I will discuss in this book had different contexts for their own encounters with Radical Inclusivity, but two general characteristics of these encounters appear to remain consistent.

First, there is the recognition that everything is included. This means not just everything I know of or can imagine is included, but everything known, unknown, and even unimaginable is included. Inclusivity doesn't become radical until it truly goes this far. My recognition of inclusivity in meditation didn't become radical until I realized that absolutely everything and anything that I could ever experience would already be included in the infinite set of "things that already are the way they are." Only then did I experience the complete surrender of any and all effort to manipulate my experience.

The second characteristic common to all experiences of Radical Inclusivity is that the recognition of it in one context leads to the uncanny sense that it applies to all contexts. There is a universality to that experience that leaves you with the undeniable sense that you are getting a glimpse into the nature of reality itself, not just the truth about one particular situation.

In this book I explore the nature of Radical Inclusivity and some of the ways that we can practice the Art of Staying on the Inside. This practice brings us over and over again to a realization of total inclusivity and the direct recognition that nothing is excluded from that. Nothing is ultimately outside. Everything is contained within an unimaginable wholeness that has no outside. We live on the inside of everything.

To be able to embrace the strangeness of this way of experiencing we have to unlearn a great deal of what we take for granted. To embrace a completely new sensibility in this way we must to be able to practice the willing suspension of disbelief[4] and pierce through layers of interpretation that have become fused with our perception of reality. I believe that the experience and exploration of Radical Inclusivity is a doorway into a new awareness that will allow us to effectively operate at new levels of consciousness. In the next chapter we will look more specifically at exactly what we can do to bring ourselves to the experience of Radical Inclusivity.

---

[4] This phrase was used by the eighteenth-century Romantic poet Samuel Taylor Coleridge in an attempt to preserve the possibility of fantasy in literature during a time when it was threatened by a growing intolerance toward any fanciful elements in writing.

CHAPTER TWO

THE ART OF STAYING ON THE INSIDE

Jeff Carreira

What I am calling the Art of Staying on the Inside is a transformative practice that involves a self-induced shift in perspective from an external and objective point of view to an internal and subjective one. To put it another way, the Art of Staying on the Inside is the practice that allows us to continuously embrace the truth that Radical Inclusivity is the way it always already is.

All of the radicalness is contained in the phrase "always already." Radical Inclusivity is the truth before we realize it and whether we realize it or not, and therefore the experience of it always comes in the form of an immediate shift in perspective. It is a jump through hyperspace into another universe, the realization of a new consciousness that appears without the elapsing of time or the traversing of space.

The experience of Radical Inclusivity exists here and now. When we find ourselves in it we realize that it was here all along and always will be. In a moment we will explore how the characteristic of always alreadyness is also associated with the experience of enlightenment as taught in many Eastern mystical schools. It also means that no practice could ever take you there because you are already there.

What is the Art of Staying on the Inside? It cannot be a practice that takes you to the consciousness of Radical Inclusivity because you are already there. The Art of Staying on the Inside is any practice that can lead you to the recognition that you are already there. That means it is a practice or contemplation that makes it possible, if not likely, that you will realize that the experience you are having is already the experience of Radical Inclusivity. That means the experience you are having right now reading this book is already it.

If the new consciousness already exists here and now, that means it is already the experience that you are having while you read these words. You cannot do anything to have the experience because you are already having it. The Art of Staying on the Inside is a way to trick yourself into the direct recognition of where you already are. It is not an effort to help you get somewhere else. It is a mechanism that gets you to stop denying that the experience you are having is already it.

Reading this might bring up feelings of disbelief. How can *this* already be *it*? This is the same consciousness that I have always been experiencing, you might think. It is what I was experiencing yesterday, last week, and a decade ago.

Yes, that's it; now you're getting it. This isn't just it now because you realize it now. This has always been it and always will be, whether you realize it or not.

Why, then, do I need to do anything at all to experience it? you could ask.

Precisely. Nothing you could do would bring you any closer to where you already are.

The Art of Staying on the Inside is a contemplative practice of inquiry. In Hindu philosophies, practices of this type are called jnana yoga or the path of wisdom. Contemplating the fact that the new consciousness we seek is already here and now is itself one form of the practice of staying on the inside. That contemplation will lead you over and over again to the realization that the consciousness you seek is already here, here, here, here, here, and here. The consciousness that you are looking for is the one looking. This experience of absolute immediacy is another quality that is always associated with Radical Inclusivity.

As you inquire on the nature of the always already quality of Radical Inclusivity, you will find that your mind keeps kicking out exceptions. That is what minds steeped in duality do when confronted with a reality that has no exceptions. They search, often frantically, for exceptions that prove the opposite.

In the face of the possibility that the new consciousness is already here and now, our minds keep pointing to aspects of our existing consciousness that appear to be exceptions that prove the statement false. "Look at this part of your awareness," it will say. "This can't possibly be the new consciousness."

During inner dialogs of this type, both the part of your mind that is making the arguments and the part that is listening to them are rooted in dualistic thinking. From that consciousness, the arguments sound very convincing, but just because they sound convincing doesn't mean they are right.

Here in lies the problem of pursuing a new level of

consciousness. It has to be done using the only tool we have—our current level of consciousness. And that tool is woefully inadequate to the task. Luckily, as inadequate as our minds might be there seems to be enough evidence to prove that we can accomplish it anyway.

Some of the traditions of Eastern enlightenment have captured the essence of the problem by asking the question, How can the mind be used to go beyond the mind?

How do we use our existing level of consciousness to propel us to the next? How do we pick ourselves up by our own bootstraps?

Unfortunately, even asking questions like this is misleading because they all rest firmly in the prior assumption that the new consciousness exists somewhere other than here. When we use phrases like "go beyond," "propel us," and "pick ourselves up," we always imply that some space will be traveled and some time will elapse between where we are and wherever we imagine we are going to end up.

Radical Inclusivity only exists here and now, and the only means of arriving is the recognition that you are already there. The consciousness that is reading these words is already it.

Tell yourself that. Tell yourself sincerely that this is it. Your mind will likely say, no it isn't, because a dualistic mind understands only in terms of a polarity between here and there and cannot understand how we can go from here to there without some process having taken us through time. The realization of Radical Inclusivity, like the Eastern realization of enlightenment, cannot happen through any process that takes time because it is taking us to where we already are.

We said that the Art of Staying on the Inside is the art of realizing that you are already on the inside. It is the art of not giving yourself license to define yourself as being outside of where you already are. In the case of the absolute immediacy that we have been describing, it means that you are already here. And the way to stay on the inside of here is by not defining any aspect of our current experience as being "not it."

This is the essence of every form of the Art of Staying on the Inside. In one way or another, depending on circumstance and context, it always involves breaking the habit of seeing some aspect of our experience as "not it." It is a practice of Radical Inclusivity because it is the practice of not excluding anything. The context and form of the contemplation can change, but its essence is always a practice of deliberate and radical inclusivity.

The quality of absolute immediacy is always associated with Radical Inclusivity, and absolute immediacy means recognizing that we are already here and always were.

Earlier we borrowed the concept of hyperspace from science fiction to help us understand how such a journey to now could take place. Another metaphor, this time from theoretical cosmology, that is even more helpful in understanding the Art of Staying on the Inside is the idea of wormholes in space.

A wormhole is an immediate connection between universes. It is like a trapdoor out of this universe and into another. It has been speculated that black holes might be trapdoors of this type. The movement from one universe to another through a wormhole is immediate and instantaneous, just like travel through hyperspace.

The difference between the two is that travel through hyperspace is still something you do that requires a hyperdrive to accomplish. A wormhole is an access point between dimensions. It is a place where two universes connect beyond time and space. Science fiction authors have speculated that we might someday map all of the wormholes in space and use them to travel freely from one universe to another.

The different forms of the Art of Staying on the Inside are like wormholes in consciousness. They are points of direct access that connect our existing level of consciousness to the next.[5] The metaphor of a wormhole is helpful because it removes any sense of effort being made. The Art of Staying on the Inside is not so much a practice that takes us from one consciousness to another. It is more of a way to play in a particular place in consciousness that we know is located near a wormhole. The idea would be that if we play in such an area long enough we will eventually fall into the wormhole by mistake and find ourselves in a new universe.

My realization of Radical Inclusivity and the conception of the Art of Staying on the Inside have a great many parallels to the Hindu tradition known as Advaita Vedanta. This is because my spiritual teacher, whose guidance I was under when I had the experience, had his own awakening in that tradition, and it was the essence of what he taught.

The goal of Advaita Vedanta is the realization of spiritual freedom, and the entire philosophy rests on

---

[5] Dr. Timothy Morton feels that finding trapdoors through consciousness of this type is critical for human beings to transcend our current level of consciousness.

the assumption that freedom is already your natural state. The goal is to be free, and free is what you already are. The essential teaching of Advaita Vedanta is to recognize that you are already free and always were. There is nowhere to go and nothing to do to become free, because free is what you already are. You cannot get there from here, because here is already there.

The pursuit of this path of awakening often occurs in the form of *satsang*, which means sitting in the presence of an awakened master. The form that satsang often takes is students asking questions of the master. Inevitably the questions will be different reasons why the student believes that he or she is not already free. The master will answer with different variations of insistence that they are.

The master's grounding in his or her own realization of freedom and the force of conviction behind it can awaken the student to their own already free nature. We might say for the benefit of our current discussion that the master has pushed the student into a wormhole in consciousness that gave them direct access to a new universe. Episodes like these can be utterly life transforming.

The goal is the realization of Radical Inclusivity. The form in this case is the contemplation of our already free nature. Our minds do not believe that we are already free, and so when introduced to this idea they respond to the challenge by looking for exceptions that prove it wrong. The mind stands in a prior attitude of disbelief of anything that does not neatly fit into its current understanding of reality. Obviously right or false until proven right is its motto.

The skeptical nature of our rational minds developed over time for very good reasons. One of the main reasons is to allow our minds to play the all-important function of holding us in a single conception of reality.[6] Ordinarily, this is obviously very good. After all, none of us want to hop around from one reality to the next with no way of relating them to each other. A person in such a state would be completely dysfunctional.

In our pursuits of higher consciousness, however, this function of the mind is problematic because it judges the validity of all new experiences and understandings against the criteria that they must fit into our current reality. If we are pursing a new reality, this can be extremely unhelpful. In our efforts to enter into the new universe of Radical Inclusivity, the automatic functioning of the mind will often not be of any use to us.

The Art of Staying on the Inside demands that we become willing and able to embrace experiences and conclusions that often seem weird, strange, and nonsensical. Practicing the willing suspension of disbelief will serve us well.

We must find a way to expand our minds beyond the acceptable into the unacceptable. This is why Dr. Timothy Morton has said that he believes philosophers should get out of the business of telling people what is real and into the business of providing

---

[6] The German philosopher Immanuel Kant was one of the first to articulate this when he described how we are held in a "transcendental unity of apperception," which we will explore more deeply in the next few pages.

philosophical Benadryl that will ease our allergic reaction to everything that seems weird, strange, and nonsensical.[7]

Any art form occurs in a medium. Painting is done in watercolors, acrylics, or oils. Sculptures are made of clay, stone, or metal. Poetry is written in language. The Art of Staying on the Inside occurs through inquiries into consciousness. This can be in the form of solitary inquiry of thought or the collective inquiry of dialog and discourse.

There are certain inquires that can be designed in such a way that they keep you in the general mental vicinity of a wormhole that leads to another universe in consciousness. By employing our minds to work on these inquires we place our awareness at the mouth of a wormhole, making it likely that we will eventually fall in if we keep the investigation going long enough.

As the exploration of this book continues, we will explore different inquires that provide this opportunity. The meditation instruction "Let everything be as it is" was the first example of such an opportunity that we explored. By tenaciously struggling with these instructions we create a high likelihood of falling into a wormhole that leads to the universe of Radical Inclusivity. We could add to this other spiritual practices, like the use of Zen koans that perform a similar function. Later we will add to the list of wormhole inquires William James' vision of the stream of consciousness and his philosophy of radical empiricism, and Gregory Bateson's

---

[7] Dr. Morton made this comment to me during a radio interview that I conducted with him.

understanding of relationship as the basis of reality. Before moving on to more specific examples, however, I want to present the general contours of the various forms of the Art of Staying on the Inside. As I already said, they invariably involve some level of inquiry that takes the general shape of realizing that there is a category from which nothing can ever be excluded. The meditation instruction of "things already as they are" is one such example of an all-inclusive category. The goal of the Art of Staying on the Inside is to put yourself in a space in consciousness in which this all inclusiveness is so obvious that it can no longer be denied.

The inquiry will begin with an all-inclusive assertion of truth, or an inquiry based on an all-inclusive assertion of truth. These assertions of truth point toward facts that are already true, always have been true, and never could be otherwise—even though we don't experience it that way. Your mind, trained as it is in the art of exclusivity, when confronted with such a fact will frantically attempt to find an exception so that it can maintain a balanced sense of duality. The possibility of all inclusivity agitates our minds until they find an exception that is excluded. At this point our minds relax.

When you assign your mind the task of allowing everything to be as it is, you are giving it a job to do that which is always already done. It is impossible to do something that is already done, but your mind will keep working at it with more and more intensity so that it can convince itself it is making headway on the task. Your mind is like a machine that will always attempt to do any task that is assigned to it. If the task is one that is always already complete, it will contort reality to create a sense of having something that lies outside of already complete so that it has something else to keep it busy.

Tying your mind up in an impossible task somewhere in the general vicinity of an all-inclusive fact makes us more susceptible to falling into the mouth of a wormhole that leads to the realization of Radical Inclusivity. And that is the Art of Staying on the Inside. Keeping your attention on a mind that is locked in an impossible inquiry at the edge of a wormhole makes it likely that eventually you will fall in. Solving the impossible puzzle is not the point; the insolubility of the task assigned is exactly what holds our attention near the wormhole long enough to make it likely that we fall in.

The challenge of this kind of spiritual practice is that you have to perch at exactly the right balance of involvement with the inquiry. If you become overly invested in solving the riddle, you will give up as soon as you realize that it is impossible. If you are too clever and realize that answering the riddle is not the point, you will not be actively engaged with it enough to keep yourself in the danger zone.

The Art of Staying on the Inside is a spiritual practice designed to keep us dancing near the edge of a wormhole that leads to a new universe in consciousness. The goal of the practice is to accidentally fall through the wormhole and wake up in a new reality. The reason we have to be so tricky about it is because our minds have been conditioned by our current reality and will attempt to hold us in it at all costs. Even if we knew exactly where the wormhole was our minds would never let us walk right into them. So we use transformational practices that keep us dancing near enough to the mouth of a wormhole to make it likely that we will fall in. The continuation of our journey requires us to explore the limits of our dualistically conditioned minds to gain a better understanding of the level of mental flexibility that makes the journey to where we already are possible.

CHAPTER THREE

THE EXPANSION OF MIND

Jeff Carreira

Immanuel Kant articulated a magnificent vision of how the human mind keeps us contained within a single worldview. Kant realized that we don't see the world as it is. Instead we see a world that is created by our minds from the selective filtering of experience. We see a phenomenal world in which disparate elements have been carefully selected and arranged to fit together according to the dictates of such constraints as the notions of time, space, and causality.

Only experiences and information that fit into our current set of universal categories is allowed to enter into consciousness. Everything else is ignored so that effectively we don't even experience it. Our minds hold us in a single reality by only allowing us to be conscious of those experiences that fit into our current conscious and unconscious beliefs about reality. In Kant's own terminology, we maintain what he called a "transcendental unity of apperception." [8]

---

[8] Immanuel Kant was a German philosopher who articulated this vision of a transcendental unity of apperception in his classic text *The Critique of Pure Reason*, first published in 1781. His

To further articulate this vision I want to invoke yet another science fiction metaphor, the holodeck from the Star Trek universe. In the television series (and movies) the crew of the starship Enterprise spend years in deep space exploring the farther reaches of the universe and having adventures. For recreation on these long voyages they had developed a magnificent device called a holodeck.

The holodeck is a large room with white walls, ceiling, and floor. The room is actually a computerized virtual reality generator. When programmed to generate a particular setting—a saloon in a frontier town of the American Old West, a sandy beach in the Bahamas, or a festival in a medieval castle—it produces a virtual replica of that reality within its white walls.

One of the amazing things about the holodeck is that it creates an unlimited world within a limited space. When you are watching a jousting match at the medieval festival, you do not experience the physical constraints of the white walls of the room you are in.

The seemingly infinite virtual reality of the holodeck is produced by perceptual trickery. The whole time that you are interacting within the virtual world inside the holodeck the program is gently shifting the image of reality that you are experiencing so that you never actually hit any of the walls. Your mind and body obey the dictates of the virtual phenomenal world that you are in so that even though in actuality you are walking in slow circles

---

conception of a world split between noumenon (the essence of things in themselves that cannot be experienced) and phenomenon (the sensual quality of things that we do experience) has dominated our experience of reality ever since.

around a big white room, you experience yourself crossing miles of rolling hills walking toward a medieval castle.

The analogy is already clear. Your mind creates a virtual reality that you exist in not knowing what, if anything, is behind it. We never see the white walls of the holodeck so far as we know what we appear to be experiencing is reality. Imagine if you had been born and lived your whole life in a holodeck programmed to imitate the circumstance of your life, and then one day the computer shut down and you found yourself in a huge white room with white walls. That would be really weird.

There are many modern-day philosophers who take this as a good analogy for how we experience reality. I don't know of any who believe that we are actually living inside something like a holodeck, although some come pretty close.[9] It is fairly common today to believe that the reality we experience is created from the synaptic snap, crackle, and pop in our brains. What is really real are the electrochemical connections in our brain, and from those the virtual reality of our phenomenal world is generated.

There are other present day philosophers who disagree. One group in particular is promoting a view called speculative realism, which we will discuss in more detail later. They disagree with the view that the

---

[9] Thomas Metzinger is a German philosopher who published a book called *The Ego Tunnel: The Science of the Mind and the Myth of the Self* in 2009. In his book he describes the effect of the ego tunnel very much like the effect of the holodeck. As he sees it, we are all living in a virtual reality generated by our minds. That is a view of reality held explicitly by many and implicitly by many more.

real world is one that exists outside of, and separate from, our experience. In different ways they are promoting the idea that the real world is already available and already inherent in our experience. It is just that the world is so different from what we think about it that we don't see it, even though we are experiencing it all the time.

Returning to the starship Enterprise, we find that our fellow crewmembers in the holodeck are in touch with reality. Their feet are hitting the real white floor, and the light in their eyes is coming from the real white walls. The fact that they experience themselves to be in a castle in the twelfth century with no experience of the white floor and walls doesn't mean that they are not in contact with them all the time. Perhaps if you started to suspect that you were trapped inside of the virtual reality contained in the holodeck you might be able to devise ways to figure that out. To do that you would need to bypass the appearance of reality so that you could come into contact with the reality underneath. This is essentially what we all have to do if we want to find the deeper realities that lie hidden behind the habitual appearances of reality.

Here we find another wormhole into the universe of Radical Inclusivity. It comes in the form of the assertion that we are always already in touch with reality. Reality isn't out there separated from us by the unbridgeable gap of our phenomenal experience. The real world is in here already. It is inside of our present experience, perhaps contorted and hidden from view but right here already and all along.

To illuminate the already-in-contact-with-reality form of Radical Inclusivity let's continue with another analogy, one of my personal favorites, a lamppost. I call this the life-under-a-lamppost analogy. Imagine a lamppost on a pitch-black night. The light from the lamppost shines down in a cone shape making a bright circle on the ground. Everything within that cone we can see; everything outside of it we can't.

Human life for most of us is generally lived under a lamppost of sorts. The cone of light within which we can see things is a metaphor for what we know and can know. The things I see under the lamppost are what I know. If there are objects under the lamppost that are out of my view behind other objects, these are the things that I don't know but could know. These are known unknowns. For instance, I don't know what is in the box in front of me, but I know if I open it I will find out. I don't know what the population of Athens is, but I know that it is there to be known. So the population of Athens is something that I know that I don't know, and I also know that I can find out if I want to.

All of the darkness that lies outside of the cone is the domain of the unknown unknowns. These things that I not only don't know, but also don't know that I don't know, don't show up for me at all. They are simply nonexistent to me. Reality for people living under such a cone (which is all of us) is defined by the cone of light that they live under. They don't see the darkness beyond the cone as unexplored reality; they just don't see it as existing. The edge of the cone is the edge of reality, and, like the holodeck, our minds create a phenomenal experience that make sure no part of us ever passes through the edge of the darkness. Those who accidentally fall over the edge will sound crazy when they try to describe their experience to anyone else in the cone. In this book I am suggesting that our experience of reality contains invisible edges that our current habits of mind will not let us cross. I am also suggesting that there are ways we can discover and travel across these edges that are impossible to understand.

The first miracle available to people living in the cone is the chance that we might find ourselves having crossed over into the darkness of nonexistence only to find that reality already exists out there. Those few who accidentally fall outside of the boundary of the known discover that the world of the cone, which had once been everything, is a very small part of a much larger reality. If they have the courage to wander around in the darkness, they find that they have infinite reaches of reality to explore. They may never be able to effectively share what they have discovered with others in the cone, but nonetheless it is there to explore.

The life-under-a-lamppost analogy doesn't get radical until we realize that even while our minds appeared to be limited by the cone of light they were already expanded beyond it into the darkness. Although we were hypnotized into experiencing only what was under the lamppost, our minds were all the while wandering out in the darkness without us. This is where things get really weird, so I may need to back up for a moment and find a different entry point.

I find it best to anchor weirdness in experience wherever possible, so now I return to the realization I had that there is a part of me that is always aware even if I am not aware of it.

My realization of perpetual consciousness occurred during the last meditation on the thirty-fourth day of retreat. On that night I was so tired that my eyes were watering, my head was aching, my muscles were stiff, and my mind felt as thick as mud. But I was determined that I was not going to fall asleep. Then a thought went through my head that said, "You're not actually tired." And I realized that in spite of how obviously false this seemed, it was also totally true. At that instant something very powerful happened in my awareness. I still had exactly the same sensations, but I had shifted into an awareness of those sensations of being tired from a place that was totally awake.

I realized that if I had slept for ten hours and was completely refreshed, opening the curtains to a bright sunny morning, the awareness that was seeing that sunny morning would not be any more awake than the awareness that was looking at the inside of a very tired mind and body. I realized that awareness is always 100 percent on and that I am never any more or less awake and aware than that. There is no way to turn awareness down. I am always awake.

When I went to sleep later, I lay down on my back and closed my eyes and felt a numbness starting at my feet and moving up my legs, engulfing me like a cocoon. I felt a mild vibration and realized that I had fallen asleep, but I hadn't lost consciousness. I thought, "Oh my God, I'm asleep." I fell deeper into sleep. My breathing became rhythmic, and I realized that I couldn't move. Eventually I lost all sensation of my body and was aware only of blackness.

In the middle of this blackness a scene emerged in front of my eyes. I quickly realized I was dreaming and that my mind had activated, obliterating the blackness and replacing it with a scene that felt as real as anything I had ever experienced. It involved a gas station and men chanting to me, but the content of it was irrelevant. What was so magnificent was the total reality of it. It felt, smelled, and looked totally real. There was no way to tell that it was otherwise.

When the mind was asleep, I was in blackness, and when the mind woke up, it was as if someone had turned on a light and a dream erupted. Then, just as suddenly as the scene had appeared, it disappeared again, and I returned to the blackness. That went on through the night until the morning, when the alarm went off and I felt my body wake up. I thought, "Now I'm awake, whatever that means."

There was no difference between sleeping, dreaming, and waking. I was the continuous thread of awareness that had watched the process of falling asleep, was aware throughout the night, and had woken up in the morning. In the morning I thought, "This is exactly what's going to happen when I die. It will be one continuous stream. I will have a body; then the body will fall away; and I will return to the blackness of pure consciousness."

From this point forward in the retreat I found myself continuously swimming in a state of Radical Inclusivity, centered on the recognition that I am always awake and always have been. The weirdness, of course, is that I don't have to be aware of being aware in order to be aware. I am awake at all times whether I realize it or not. The unavoidable question to be answered was, What was it that was always awake if I am not aware of it?

I don't know how valuable an experience like this is at giving us an accurate picture of reality. Their real value is that they open up our minds and liberate our imagination. My experience of ongoing immersion in Radical Inclusivity opened up avenues of inquiry that would have been simply impossible before. Unimaginable questions now seemed valid to ask and ponder.

A vision of reality began to congeal in me that was very strange indeed. The experience of being awake was not something that happened inside of me; it was a quality of reality itself. Awareness didn't live in my mind or body; it lived in reality. It is not me that is aware; it is reality that is aware through me. Imagine that the entire universe has as part of its being the capacity to be aware. What dictates the experience of awareness at any spot in the universe is whatever form exists there, because different forms have unique capacities for experiencing awareness.

More typically we imagine that our experience of awareness is being generated inside of us. If I walk across the room, I see a different perspective on the room, and I assume that the scene has shifted because awareness is inside of me and I have shifted. I am the source of awareness, and so when I move, the scene shifts. What I now began to suspect was that the awareness of different perspectives of the room does not exist in me. They are there in reality waiting for a set of eyeballs to come along. All perspectives exist simultaneously always in reality. When I walk across the room, I am not carrying the source of awareness over there to see from that angle; I am moving my visual apparatus over there so that I can enliven the perspective that lives over there. When I walk away from that spot, the perspective stays there, waiting for the next pair of eyeballs to come and enliven it again.

Awareness does not exist in me. It exists

everywhere all the time. There is a particular human experience of awareness that only comes alive through a human being, but awareness itself exists already waiting to spring into being when it comes into contact with a human form. An analogy that will help us get a handle on something so strange is a radio. You might imagine that a child might falsely assume that the music was coming out of the radio because they do not yet realize that the music is being carried on radio waves that exist in the atmosphere all around. The radio transforms those waves into sound, but the radio is not the source of the sound. In a similar way, awareness is alive as a field that we exist within all the time. We are not the source of awareness even though the awareness comes to a particular fruition when it comes in contact with us.

On the meditation retreat we sat in rows and meditated with our eyes slightly open in the Buddhist style. Throughout the rest of the retreat I kept realizing that it no longer made sense to me why I could only see through the eyes associated with my body. If awareness existed everywhere, why did I seem only to be privy to the experience of the awareness coming into contact with this body? It just didn't make sense. The awareness existed everywhere; what was connecting me to only this one spot?

The obvious answer is because I am attached to this body. But what is the "I" that is attached? I would have thought it was awareness. I had thought that the source of awareness was in my body and brain, but now it was clear to me that this was not the case. So what was the nature of an "I" that could be attached to a body? The only thing that made any sense to me was that the limitation of only experiencing the sensation of one body was just a habit of perception that existed in reality itself and was so strong that it could not be broken. I was convinced that if I could let go enough I would be flooded with the experiences of everyone else. That never happened, thank God.

As the days of retreat unfolded, I became more and more grounded in the understanding that I did not exist and had never existed in the way that I had imagined I had. The idea that I was an individual person who was born into a body and lived my life and would eventually die was just a fiction that was perpetuated by the force of habit. This does not mean that there is no me that exists. I believe that there is an essence to all of us that has a unique relationship to a particular mind and body, but it does not live inside of that mind and body. Like radio waves in the air, the essence of who I am exists everywhere at once. My mind and body is the radio that has been specifically tuned to receive and transmit my particular essence. It is a radio tuned to only one frequency, but the frequency exists everywhere.

My experiences on retreat had propelled me far outside of any cone of light that I had been living under. I was now out in the blackness beyond the perimeter of the known, discovering things that were unknowable under the lamppost. As this book continues, I will share more of what I have contemplated and discovered during and since that time, but what is most important is not the conclusions that I may have come to, but the freedom to think this wildly and freely yourself—to allow your mind to expand beyond all constraints of the known and slip outside of the transcendental unity of apperception.

Later, as I began an earnest study of philosophy, I discovered that Romantic thinkers like Samuel Taylor Coleridge and Ralph Waldo Emerson also believed that the source of awareness was a field of pure reason ready to spring into knowledge and understanding at any instant. Eventually I discovered the writings of the American philosophers Charles Sanders Peirce and William James and learned how they were both attempting in different ways to articulate a similar vision of reality. And in the past decade a small group of present-day philosophers have embarked on a project to establish speculative realism as a new force in philosophy that gives validity to speculations this wild and free.

I now see that what I was opened up to through the prolonged experience of Radical Inclusivity is a state of wildly unbounded speculation about what is real. Inquiry of this type follows in the intellectual footsteps of Peirce and James and finds companionship today among the speculative realists, who endeavor to make wild speculation about the nature of reality acceptable and even fashionable again.

The contemplation of just how far out our thinking can get is itself a form of the Art of Staying on the Inside. We live within a vast expanse of the unknown and unknowable. Think about that. It is not too hard to imagine that there are aspects of reality that you don't know. It is harder to really let in that there are aspects to reality that you can't know—that your mind in its current state, trapped as it is in a holodeck of virtual reality, cannot grasp. It is even harder to imagine that the aspects of reality that you cannot know are already within your experience. Your mind already extends into the realms that you cannot know. This is all very, very strange. It demands a complete revisioning of reality, but that investigation will have to wait until our next chapter.

The form of Radical Inclusivity that we have been discussing here is born out of the recognition that we live within a mystery that is both beyond our comprehension and already within our minds. Our deepest experiences of spiritual awakening often lead us to this recognition. I remember in the middle of the experience of perpetual consciousness that I described earlier I was standing outside looking at the sky. I realized that I had no idea what was really going on here. The movie *The Truman Show*[10] came to mind, and I started to see the entire seen in front of me like a dome with a picture of a sky and a landscape on it. And I realized that I could be living in a holodeck and wouldn't ever know it.

One of the problems with everything I have shared with you in this chapter is that it is still held captive within the hypnotic power of a Cartesian and Newtonian view of reality. In other words, it presupposes a universe of infinite empty space filled with separate objects that affect one another through force. The metaphors of the holodeck, the lamppost and the radio, as I have described them still all exist in an assumed realty that I like to refer to as a things-in-space reality. Our minds are so conditioned to see

---

[10] In the movie *The Truman Show*, the main character comes to discover that his whole life has been staged as part of a television production. The little town he lives in exists in reality as a huge set built under a dome, and everyone in his life is an actor in the show.

everything in terms of things-in-space that it is impossible to see any other way, but if we really want to expand our minds beyond the edges of the known we have to try to leave our things-in-space mentality behind us. That is the journey we will begin in the next chapter.

CHAPTER 4

THINGS-IN-SPACE CONSCIOUSNESS

We are discussing the possibility of moving into a new reality through experiences of Radical Inclusivity that can be self-induced through the Art of Staying on the Inside. Eventually any discussion of a new reality must confront the obvious challenge that we are trying to get there from where we are. That means that all of the tools that might help us are still anchored in the old reality, and inevitably they must also be left behind. The shift from one reality to the next must be an immediate and discontinuous jump that results in a new reality that completely and instantaneously replaces the old one with no time elapsed and no space traversed.

The challenge is that we are always living inside an existing worldview, and the only language we have to help guide us to the edge of a wormhole will itself be inside of our existing worldview. In order to give way to a new possibility we have to let go of everything that tethers us to the old way of being. Everything we might use to move us to a new way of being will be a connection back to the old. Everything we use to try to disconnect ourselves from the old will itself be a part of the old. This is similar to the experience I described of trying to follow the meditation instructions of letting everything be as it is. Anything I tried to do to let everything be as it is would itself be a way of trying to change things, which is not letting them be as they are.

Earlier I said that metaphors and analogies can be very useful in guiding our thinking along our journey into the unknowable, but even metaphors and analogies have their limits. Inevitably every metaphor and every analogy will be bound to our current worldview, so in the end they become merely a more subtle form of bondage and not a means to escape. In order to learn how to loosen our metaphors and analogies from our current worldview it will be helpful to explore what that worldview is.

We are essentially living within what is generally known as the modern worldview. The problem with worldviews can be seen even in the naming of them. The label *modern* implies current. The modern worldview is current only in comparison to the one before, but not to the one that will come after. Every worldview sees only from its own perspective, and therefore in the case of modernism it sees itself as the end of history, the fruition of time, not as a brief resting place along an infinite chain of being. Naming our worldview *modern* leads to the awkward use of the term *postmodern* as an attempt to name what comes next. Of course the use of the term *postmodern* is born out of the modern worldview and therefore labels the next stage of development in relationship to itself. You probably see already the Radical Inclusivity implied here. Everything we think and everything we do will already be modern, even if we are attempting to think, see, and act beyond it.

The modernist worldview was born during the Age of Enlightenment that spread through Europe during the sixteenth and seventeenth centuries. This was a time during which the classical worldview of the Middle Ages was supplanted by the modernist worldview that we remain largely embedded in today.

It is difficult and perhaps impossible for us to fully grasp the reality of the Middle Ages. The leap that occurred in human consciousness during the Age of Enlightenment is nothing short of miraculous. Imagine being alive during The Middle Ages. Your entire understanding of the world, if you had any at all, was made up of a combination of Christian doctrine sprinkled with Aristotelian logic and superstition. From a modern point of view it was as if you didn't understand anything at all—at least not in anything like the way we understand things.

When the plagues hit, you would have no idea why three-quarters of the people around you were dying. You would probably conclude that either evil spirits were attacking and/or God was punishing humanity for some regression. You would never imagine that the lack of cultural norms around personal hygiene could almost entirely account for the source of the problem.

The Middle Ages was a time undoubtedly dominated by fear. The same God who mysteriously provided you with the earth under your feet, air to breathe, and food to eat also left you riddled with disease and ill health, and periodically subjected you to natural and human disasters of all kinds. There was no clear way to act that would accurately allow you to predict or control the future, so the God you worshiped was an impossible mix of benevolence and cruelty.

The most learned people of the time created a worldview by synthesizing knowledge found in Greek texts with Christian doctrine that held the Western world together during its bleakest period in history. The worldview of the "medieval synthesis," as it came to be known, remained intact until the Polish astronomer Nicholaus Copernicus pulled the rug out from under it.

Copernicus showed convincingly that the Earth revolved around the Sun and not the Sun around the Earth. This discovery overthrew one of the central tenets of Christian thought and spurred arguably the greatest intellectual revolution in human history. Soon the German astronomer Johannes Kepler showed that the planets revolved around the Earth according to simple mathematical relationships, and later the Englishman Isaac Newton revealed the source of planetary movement using a simple and elegant theory of gravity.

The Enlightenment changed the universe. Suddenly it was clear that the universe wasn't an unknowable place to be feared. It was an organized mechanism consisting of many different parts that acted according to natural laws that could be discovered and understood. The universe was knowable, and our minds were perfectly suited to know it. That was the revolution of the Enlightenment.

The new universe that emerged looked like a clockwork that operated according to laws that could be discovered, understood, and controlled. There was a utopian impulse that erupted among Enlightenment thinkers because they had discovered the key to perfecting the world.

The Enlightenment gave us a new way to understand reality. Medieval cosmology was a vision of moving solid spheres that surrounded our earth, separating us from the white light of heaven beyond. The stars we saw at night were perforations in the heavenly spheres that allowed heaven's light to shine through.

The consciousness of the Enlightenment was built on a completely different cosmology. Reality consists of an infinite space of three dimensions. This is the Cartesian space that we learned about in school. It is an infinite stage of empty space filled with things. We all tend to relate to ourselves as things in space. We see the universe as merely an expanse of vacuous nothingness—a virtual stage in which we are the intelligent actors. We see a universe that is empty and full of objects—stars, planets, mountains, buildings, cars, and toothbrushes, to name a few. And people, of course, are also objects that exist in the universe. People are unique kinds of objects because we think, feel, and perceive. We are, as Descartes once noted, thinking things.

This is the fundamental picture of reality that you and I hold. This fundamental image forms a huge part of the core of our consciousness. In different ways, gross and subtle, we see everything in terms of empty space filled with things. In fact, what we earlier called the consciousness of duality we could as easily call things-in-space consciousness, and the main occupation of that consciousness is the identification of things. One of the greatest skills we have is the ability to create separate individual things out of the undivided whole of reality. We create things by chopping the world into pieces along lines that are usually chosen for reasons of human convenience.[11]

For instance, we see a tall plant and define it as a "tree." We draw a boundary around the tree that is convenient for us in many ways but when inspected carefully isn't ultimately accurate to reality. When we look at some of the appendages sticking out of the tree, we define them as "branches." The flat green pieces that sprout out of the branches we call "leaves." And a tree becomes a compound thing made up of a trunk with some branches and leaves. Branches are things that sprout leaves. Leaves are things that grow out of branches. If you look carefully, however, you don't see sharp boundaries separating the trunk from the branches or the branches from the leaves. If we look more closely, we find that nutrients and sunlight pass in and out through the surfaces of the tree all the time. And at the level of atomic structure there is even less reason to assume any sharp boundaries separating the atoms that make up the tree from those around it.

The consciousness of things-in-space is always on the look out for lines of demarcation that separate things. One of the fundamental capacities of our minds is the ability to create distinctions where there were none before. When we make a distinction, we discover a new way to separate one thing from another. One of the fundamental modalities of things-in-space consciousness is making distinctions

---

[11] The twentieth-century anthropologist Gregory Bateson wrote and spoke often about the human habit of splitting reality into separate objects along lines of human convenience and the ecological damage caused as a result.

that divide reality into separate things.

There is another worldview, the very one we are trying to fall into, that has been emerging over at least the past century and a half. One of the key elements of this worldview is the recognition that reality is not made up of separate things in empty space: reality is one continuous whole. There are no gaps or breaks in reality.

Describing the universe as an interconnected whole doesn't capture the true level of continuity that actually exists in our universe. The universe is not a collection of separate things that are all touching at their edges. It is a universe that doesn't contain separate things or edges at all. It is a universe without separation. And yet it is not an undifferentiated whole either. Later in the book we will examine how it might be possible to think of such a strange universe, but first we must go a little more deeply into the realm of continuity.

Charles Darwin's publication of *On the Origin of Species* delivered a mortal wound to the things-in-space view of reality. Continuity is the core of Darwin's conception of species transmutation. In his book, Darwin writes that after studying bird species closely he was "much struck how entirely vague and arbitrary is the distinction between species and varieties." He goes on to say, "The term species thus comes to be a mere useless abstraction, implying and assuming a separate act of creation."

What Darwin recognized was that we think of species as well-defined separate life forms with clear boundaries between them, but in fact the line that separates one species from the next is often blurry and at times arbitrary. A species is really an abstract idea constructed from an imagined set of characteristics that often don't appear in reality as distinctly as we imagine them to be.

Darwin began to see that animal species fall within a continuum in which one species seems to blur into the next. He realized—although he found it difficult to accept at first—that each species was not created independently. They developed one into the next in the chain of development called evolution. This, coupled with his theory of natural selection, which explained how this change could occur without an outside intelligence to guide it, made his ideas as revolutionary as Copernicus's discovery that the Earth revolved around the Sun.

The full magnitude of the implications of Darwin's realization is difficult, nearly impossible, to grasp by the consciousness of things-in-space. Our minds are machines designed to create objects by drawing boundaries and making distinctions. These boundaries wrap at lightning speed around perceptual and functional characteristics like size, shape, color, edible, enjoyable, etc. in any combination. A thing is red and not blue, big and not small, hard and not soft. This is the consciousness of duality. It defines reality as things that are this and not that. Absolute continuity isn't understandable to things-in-space consciousness because one continuous whole defies comparison and distinction.

One of my favorite American philosophers is Charles Sanders Peirce, who in the late nineteenth century developed the ideas that would become the American philosophy called pragmatism with his friend William James. Throughout his life Peirce attempted to create a philosophy based on the assumption that everything was part of one continuous evolutionary unfolding. It is impossible to imagine total continuity for a things-in-space mind because you can never separate anything from that continuity that could stand as an understanding of it. This absolute inclusivity was for Peirce one of the primary characteristics of reality. He referred to it as "firstness," by which he meant the essence of being first, or that which exists without another. The following passage is one of my favorites from his writings because it captures the meaning of nonduality as clearly as anything I have ever read. If you read this passage and contemplate firstness carefully, you will see that it offers another wormhole edge to dance around in the hopes that you will fall in.

The idea of the absolutely First must be entirely separated from all conception of or reference to anything else; for what involves a second is itself a second to that second. The First must therefore be present and immediate, so as not to be second to a representation. It must be fresh and new, for if old it is second to its former state. It must be initiative, original, spontaneous, and free; otherwise it is second to a determining cause. It is also something vivid and conscious; so only it avoids being the object of some sensation. It precedes all synthesis and all differentiation; it has no unity and no parts. It cannot be articulately thought: assert it, and it has already lost its characteristic innocence; for assertion always implies a denial of something else. Stop to think of it, and it has flown! What the world was to Adam on the day he opened his eyes to it, before he had drawn any distinctions, or had become conscious of his own existence—that is first, present, immediate, fresh, new, initiative, original, spontaneous, free, vivid, conscious, and evanescent. Only, remember that every description of it must be false to it.

Peirce and James were inspired to create a philosophy that reflected the true continuity of reality. They had been inspired to this philosophical project by reading *On the Origin of Species* and discussing it together. In it they learned that Darwin had realized that many of the objects we take as real (specifically, in his case, different species such as the red-tailed finch) are actually perceptual categories, not actual objects. Although each member of that category is real, the category itself is an organizing tool.

The most general perceptual category is a "thing." And our mind is constantly creating things by drawing boundaries that separate certain parts of our perceptual field from the rest. That is what things-in-space consciousness does. In fact the habit of seeing reality as ultimately made up of things runs so deep that it is built right into our language (which means into our thinking.) For instance, our word for totality is *everything*, and our word for absolute lack is *nothing*. The implications are obvious. If you gathered up all the things in the universe, you would have everything there is, and if there were no things left, the universe would cease to be.

When we look more closely, we see that "things" are not as clear-cut as they may appear. The boundaries that separate things can be fuzzy and shifting. As we travel through the world, we are confronted with a constant barrage of things. Physical things that we call objects, mental things that we call ideas, emotional things that we call feelings—and all of these things are constantly shifting and morphing right in front of our eyes. At any particular moment, one thing will stand out in our attention against the background of our experience and then disappear again into the background as another thing leaps forward in perception. Each thing, be it physical, mental, or emotional, is either acted upon or not as it appears in our awareness and then returns back into the blur of shifting things and background. We get used to the constant shifting, and for convenience sake we accept many of the things that we perceive to have a reality that is more solid than it actually is.

Obviously the skill of creating things out of the field of our perception has tremendous advantages and has made all of what we know possible. At the same time it has disadvantages as well. In fact our world is suffering from some disastrous consequences of the consciousness that sees everything in terms of things-in-space and more specifically as things to be used and consumed.[12]

It is common today for people to think about the "interconnectedness" of all things, but I believe this term falls short of the true continuity of reality because it implies separate elements that are connected, which is not the same as one continuous whole. I believe that Radical Inclusivity is the closest

---

[12] There are many brilliant thinkers and authors, too numerous to mention here, that have explained in many ways exactly how our current level of consciousness is inadvertently responsible for many of the global challenges that we face today.

experience that a mind drenched in things-in-space consciousness can have of true continuity. Our minds are machines that look for edges and distinctions that separate things. When our minds find themselves on the inside of anything, they look for boundaries that split the inside from the outside so they can define an object they can grasp. Imagine the simple example of confusion. Whenever we are confused, we attempt to figure out why we are confused. That means drawing a boundary around the confusion that allows us to understand it. Understanding our confusion involves turning our experience of confusion into a conceptual object, an idea, that fits comfortably alongside all of our other ideas. We feel relief when we are able to explain our confusion as an idea that fits into our other ideas.

If a mind trained to identify things finds itself inside a space of absolute continuity, it will search relentlessly for a boundary that separates the inside from the outside. It cannot, of course, and so eventually it has to give in. Once our things-in-space mind gives up trying to find a boundary that separates the experience it is having from the rest of the world, the reality of total continuity floods in. That flood is the experience of Radical Inclusivity.

We are defining a shift from things-in-space consciousness to a consciousness I will refer to as continuity-unfolding consciousness. This is a vision of reality that our things-in-space minds cannot fully imagine. What are the characteristics of a universe that unfolds as a single continuous whole? Such a universe is absolutely full and expanding at the same time. Our things-in-space minds have trouble with this because if the universe were absolutely full there would be no room left to expand into. And that, of course, is the point. There is no room left in this universe. It is a totally full, complete, and continuous whole, and yet it is expanding and unfolding anyway.

What are we in this new universe? In a things-in-space reality we ourselves are some of the things that exist in the empty space. We imagine that we are separated by edges that isolate us from the rest of reality. In a reality of continuity unfolding, the edges that separate us fall away. How do we see ourselves if we are no longer things in space? Who are we in this new reality of continuous unfolding?

The first image that comes to my mind is an air bubble in water. The idea of separating a bubble from the water it floats in is nonsensical. The water around it defines the bubble. The bubble has no existence outside of the water. In the same way a human being is defined by its environment, and the idea of removing a human being from its environment is equally nonsensical. We do not exist outside of our environment.

The layer of life around the earth is referred to as the biosphere. Our things-in-space minds think of ourselves as things that live in the biosphere. From the point of view of continuity, a human being is more like a bubble in the biosphere similar to an air bubble in water. If, for instance, you wanted to remove an air bubble from a pond, you would have to build a container (like a jar) that holds enough water for the bubble to be held in. Similarly, if you wanted to remove a human from the biosphere, you would have to create a container (a spaceship) that holds enough biosphere for the human to be held in. A human being is not a thing that can be removed from the biosphere any more than an air bubble is a thing that can be removed from the water.

Contemplating yourself as a human bubble is a profound way to practice the Art of Staying on the Inside. We are all on the inside of our physical environment all the time. Keep imagining yourself as an air bubble. The shape you are in is not yours; the atmosphere pressing against you is holding you together, just like an air bubble. What would happen if you were suddenly to appear naked in deep space? I don't think you would recognize yourself.

How about the air you are breathing? If you wanted to travel off of the earth, you would have to take a lot of that with you. And when does the air you breath become a part of you and not a separate thing outside of you? Is the air in your lungs part of you, or is that still part of the air outside? What about the oxygen molecules that entered into your bloodstream? Are they part of you now because they are in your blood stream and not your lungs? Or is it when they are metabolized into energy that allows you to move and think? Is that where the hard line is that separates you from the outside? Or is it all inside? Are you completely and radically inside the environment?

Once I was with a friend talking about the continuity of reality when we both slipped through a wormhole into the experience of Radical Inclusivity. Suddenly it was obvious. Everything was part of this continuity. Nothing was outside of it. I remember moving my hand slowly through the air marveling at how I was no longer seeing a thing moving through empty space. Now I was seeing movement within continuity, like watching different colors of paint swirling together. No one of the colors was the thing and the others the space. It was all part of a single continuity. My hand was not a thing in space anymore. Hand and space were all part of one continuous whole.

Another time I fell through this same wormhole through another practice altogether. It was during a time when for a decade I practiced celibacy. Most of us think of celibacy as a practice of renunciation, which it is of course, but the way I was taught the act of renunciation was a context in which to contemplate the fullness of life.

Our sex drive is perhaps the strongest drive in our bodies. It is a powerful physical drive propelled by the procreative force embedded in the species as a whole. It is also a strong social drive tied inextricably in our cultural lexicon to the attainment of satisfaction and happiness. When you practice celibacy in the way that I was taught, you consciously renounce sex and in that context enter into a contemplation about what, if anything, is missing. If I don't have sex, which feels utterly essential to being full and happy, what is actually missing?

I remember the day that I realized nothing was missing. I was utterly fine, wonderful in fact, and felt no need to have sex ever again. Sex didn't appear to me as anything less than it had been before, but now the rest of the world seemed totally full and complete with or without it. I remember running around in a state of exultation asking out loud, "What is missing? Where is the hole that I think needs to be filled?" There is no hole; nothing is missing; and everything is full.

The explosive recognition that everything is already full was yet another avenue into the experience of Radical Inclusivity. It led to the recognition of total continuity by revealing that there was nothing missing in the universe, no gaps to fill. Celibacy had been a form of staying on the inside, and it had brought me to the realization that everything is already full.

The experience of Radical Inclusivity that I found myself in had nothing to do with sex. When I was running around asking, "What is missing?" any ideas about the practice of celibacy had been left behind. The realization of Radical Inclusivity that I was immersed in was only about the total fullness of life. The recognition that "everything is already full," like the realization that "everything is already the way it is," was a wormhole to a new consciousness.

The experience of Radical Inclusivity and all forms of the Art of Staying on the Inside are pointing toward a new reality and a new consciousness. In this chapter we have been exploring a conscious shift from the things-in-space consciousness that we were blessed with during the Enlightenment to the possibility of a continuity-unfolding consciousness that lies just on the other side of a wormhole. So far we have been focused mainly on continuity. Before exploring the nature of unfolding, we need to spend the duration of the next chapter exploring the furthest possibilities of speculation and deepening our understanding of things-in-space consciousness.

CHAPTER FIVE

BEYOND HUMAN PERSPECTIVES

Jeff Carreira

This short book can be seen as, and in fact in many ways is, my personal introduction to the philosophy called speculative realism. This new philosophy has only been defined and developed during the course of the last decade by a handful of pioneering thinkers. As I see it, speculative realism is creating a context for the kind of inquiry that I am advocating for in this book.

I first came into contact with this group of philosophers through the work of Dr. Timothy Morton, in the form of lectures on Romanticism that he offers through iTunes.[13] I had long realized that a great deal of alternative spiritual thought can be seen as an extension of the Romantic project of the eighteenth century, but Dr. Morton's lectures made it vividly clear to me why the Romantic emphasis on

---

[13] Timothy Morton of Rice University is the speculative realist that I have been most influenced by. Morton is the author of several books, including *Ecology Without Nature*, *The Ecological Thought*, and *Hyperobjects*. He is probably surpassed, however, by Graham Harman as the leader of this emerging movement in philosophy.

authenticity and imagination is so important to us now.

We have already explored the things-in-space conception of realty that was established during the Enlightenment. The Romantics were reacting in part to what they saw as the excessive faith in reason and rationality of the Enlightenment thinkers. They believed that humankind had developed an untenable hubris in relationship to its self-declared ability to understand everything. The Enlightenment had been built on an unshakable conviction that the entire universe was comprehensible and could be grasped in its totality by the human mind.

The Romantic thinkers felt that this excessive faith in rationality was suffocating to the human spirit. Where the Enlightenment saw a universe that was mechanical and run by fixed laws, the Romantics saw a universe that was organic and grew in accordance with acts of passion and will. The Enlightenment had held human reason and rationality in the highest regard. The Romantics held human agency and creative freedom to be sacred.

Many Romantics felt that we had lost something in our rush out of the medieval world. The thinkers of the Middle Ages, for all of their shortcomings, had at least recognized our limited ability to understand reality and had wisely left much of the universe draped in mystery and uncertainty. Perhaps in our dash out of those darker times a baby had been thrown out with the bath water. They agreed that we should strive to understand our universe, and they recognized the obvious limitations of superstition and unquestioned dogma; yet they also yearned to recapture the mystery of life. They believed that the religious tradition had pointed to an underlying truth that didn't need to be discarded, but simply rearticulated in a language of nature and growth.

With the rising success of science and rationality, metaphysical speculation began to fall out of fashion. As we moved into the twentieth century, the activity of philosophy was dominated by the same evidence-based approach to rationality that had led to so much success in science. Philosophy had all but given up on the occupation of trying to understand reality. The "linguistic turn" is a phrase used to describe a trend in philosophy that turned us away from trying to understand reality toward forms that were designed to help us understand the language we used to describe reality instead. This was an attempt to address problems of linguistics that had led to insoluble philosophical arguments about what was ultimately real for centuries. At the same time this analytic trend surfaced its own problems, and those are what the speculative realists are attempting to address.

Toward the start of the twentieth century many philosophers began to come to the conclusion that philosophy might be nothing more than debates about language. They came to this conclusion because philosophy is an attempt to expand our knowledge about what is real and true, and everything that we know about what is real and true can only be known and articulated in language. To take philosophy to the next level of debate we would need to attain a much more precise understanding of language. And so philosophy took the linguistic turn into an exploration of language and what language is capable of telling us about reality.

Many brilliant minds took up the project of

understanding the relationship between language and reality. In this effort it became increasingly clear that language alone was never going to be able to fulfill Descartes' dream of discovering a truth that did not assume anything. Language is inherently referential, which means that the meaning it expresses can only be understood against some assumed background of information. You will never be able to make a statement of truth that is entirely free of all assumptions. To some this seemed to point to the possibility that every truth was relative and nothing is ultimately real. There is no ultimate truth because all truth is relative to something that must inherently lie outside of itself.

As was mentioned earlier, Immanuel Kant had already declared that reality was ultimately unknowable by the late eighteenth century. The revelations of the linguistic turn in philosophy seemed to reveal more understanding as to why minds trafficking in language would never be able to know reality directly. We are fated to know only a phenomenal world with no ultimate certainty about the relationship our perceived reality might have to some actual reality that lies beneath it. This understanding is sometimes called a correspondence theory of mind because it sees our minds as creating a phenomenal experience of a reality that exists somewhere outside of its grasp.

This model of mind does not seem disagreeable on the surface. Most of us would readily admit that what we perceive as reality is not exactly accurate. Our perception is made up partly of things, which are objectively real, and partly of interpretations that we add to the picture. Closer inspection reveals that this simple idea leads to a disconcerting assumption of separation from the real world.

When we talk about objective reality, what we commonly mean is that which is real even if we are not around. Objective reality—or the real world—is a reality independent of us. That means if something is objectively real I will see it the same way that everyone else does. If two or more people see things differently, they can't all be seeing what is objectively real. To get to what is truly real we would have to strip away any errors in perception or biases that any one of us might be holding.

And that is the way we tend to think about reality. Reality, we imagine, is what is left when we are not adding anything extra to the picture. To get from our interpreted picture of reality to an accurate picture of reality all we need to do is strip away the interpretation and move closer and closer to the real world. We discover what is real by stripping away what is false. Reality is out there, and to see it clearly all we have to do is get out of the way. If we think about it for a moment, this implies a belief that in order to get to what is real we have to strip ourselves out of the picture, and that seems to place us outside of reality.

The inherent problems with this implied separation from reality is what drives some of the speculative realists to pursue an alternative in philosophy. Timothy Morton pointed out to me that at the same time Kant was formulating a philosophy that separated us from reality the steam engine was being developed and coming into popular use. Many ecologists see the widespread use of the steam engine as the start of human-generated degradation of our global climate. Examining the earth's crust shows that this is when measurable quantities of carbon started entering into our atmosphere. Morton claims it is no coincidence that a philosophy that separated us from reality emerged at the same time that we embarked on a path of tremendous destruction toward our ecology.

The question that must be asked is, Where does philosophy need to go from here? What kind of philosophy can put us back inside of reality? One insight of the speculative realists is that the philosophies of the twentieth century, while doing important work in pointing out the limits of human knowledge, are still fundamentally philosophies of human reality. When philosophy is exclusively concerned with what human beings know about reality, we privilege the human perspective above all other possible perspectives. Any such philosophy inherently separates the human experience from everything else. According to speculative realism, we need an understanding of reality that takes us beyond a merely human perspective of reality.

The postmodern philosophies of the twentieth century embraced all human perspectives as valid and created tremendous opportunity for many, many people. The validation of all human perspectives brought an unprecedented expanse of human rights and individual freedom. These philosophies were not, however, designed to take us beyond human perspectives. Regardless of their expansiveness they still privileged the human experience, and that favoring cannot help but hold an inherent blindness that we must move beyond.

Philosophically, a realist is someone who believes that there is a reality that exists independent of our human experience of it. Speculative realists are realists in this sense. At the same time they also recognize the inadequacies and limitations of our things-in-space minds to fully comprehend reality, especially as we move into a nonhuman-centered understanding of reality. For this reason they promote a profoundly speculative attitude in philosophy.

We have already established that reality is not bound by our current human experience. Yet our human experience is the only access point we have into reality. We must find a way to be unimaginably free and flexible with our conceptions of reality because wild speculation is the only philosophical attitude that stands a chance to envision a reality that lies beyond our experience of it. Speculative realism is an umbrella category that houses a group of wildly imaginative philosophers who have taken on the bold task of dehumanizing our perspective of reality.

What will we become when we become capable of embracing and responding from a view that extends beyond human perspectives?

This brings us back to the central thesis of this book. "Continuity unfolding" is the phrase I am using to describe the consciousness that lies beyond our current dualistic, things-in-space, human-centered consciousness. For us to be able to make the leap into this new level of consciousness we must exercise the same extreme tolerance for speculation about reality that the speculative realists are advocating. As we discussed in the opening chapters of this book, a shift in consciousness of this magnitude leads to a new reality, and there is ultimately no way to get from here to there in a straight line. We have to search for wormholes in consciousness that connect this reality to a different one. Wild philosophical speculation is yet another dance at the edge of a wormhole. Throughout history there have been a string of bold pioneering thinkers who have danced long enough at those edges to fall through to the other side.

The next thing that we need to do in this inquiry is explore some possible candidates for a continuity-unfolding view of reality. Before we do, however, it will serve us to briefly revisit the historical development of our things-in-space consciousness from a different angle.

One of the questions that philosophers worry most about is, What is real? and the answers we come to, whether through our own inquiry or in submission to the authority of others, are very important. Whatever counts as real to us is what has significance to us. It is what we care about, nurture, and protect. Everything else is a derivative and inevitably carries less significance.

Through most of human history the quest to discover what reality is made of revolved around the search for substance. The word *substance* derives from roots that could be translated to mean the "being under our feet." A substance is the real "stuff" that the rest of the universe is made from. Whatever we believe is the one substance that everything else is made of—be it atoms, energies, or God—is what ultimately counts as real.

In the last chapter we explored the things-in-space consciousness of modernism in terms of its being rooted in a vision of reality as an infinite expanse of three-dimensional space populated by things. A question that naturally arises then is, What are all the things made of? What is the "stuff" of reality?

Many of the cornerstone characteristics of the consciousness we live in are recognized to have their origins in the astoundingly original ideas of René Descartes, the French philosopher and mathematician of the early seventeenth century. We have already acknowledged Descartes' influence in establishing a vision of a universe that extends infinitely in three dimensions. Even more famously he imagined a distinction between mind and matter that dominates all of our experience of reality.

In an effort to discover what was really real, Descartes sat down, on his bed I have heard, and decided to doubt everything until he discovered something that could not be doubted. His plan was to build a picture of reality out of whatever it was that he could be absolutely sure of. His famous treatise called *Meditations on First Philosophy* is his account of the thought process that ensued.

One line of inquiry that he followed rested on the common experience of dreaming. In dreams we experience the world and ourselves very convincingly. While we lie in bed asleep and unconscious to the "real" world, we run around and act in a "dream" world as our "dream" self. Descartes wondered if his experience of normal waking reality might be a kind of dream created in his mind. You will notice that he was opening the same investigation that we opened up using the holodeck metaphor.

As he continued his meditations, he came to conclude that this was not the case. There were differences between the inner world of dreams and the outer world we live in. There were, in fact, two distinct realms of reality. One was an inner realm that we experience as mind, and the other was an outer realm that we experience as matter and world. This split between mind and matter, inner and outer has become so habitually the way we see the world that it is hard to imagine things any other way. What kind of consciousness would enable us to see mind and matter not as separate realms of reality but as aspects of one continuous whole?

In terms of the quest for substance, mind and matter are two substances that we see reality being made of. All of reality is created from these. This split and the implications it holds are often referred to as Cartesian dualism, and you don't have to look very far to see how much your experience of reality is influenced by it. Look at the world around you. Touch something. Feel it on your skin. All of that we experience as the world of matter. Now look inside. Look at your thoughts, feelings, and emotions. That is the inner world of mind. Both the outer world of matter and the inner world of mind are obvious to us, as is the fact that they represent separate dimensions of reality.

Our consciousness sits in this foundational split between mind and matter, inner and outer. It is at the very core of our experience of reality, and it is also a huge part of the duality that collapses in the experience of Radical Inclusivity. Our goal is to discover a vision of a new reality that rests on an experience of continuity unfolding, and on the way there we have to question the assumption that the inner world of mind and the outer manifestation of matter are really separate. What vision of reality can reveal mind and matter to be inextricable aspects of an unbroken continuous whole? This is the journey we will take in the next chapter, and it will prove to be a step toward a view of reality that takes us beyond human perspectives.

Jeff Carreira

CHAPTER SIX

THE REALITY OF EXPERIENCE

Long before I discovered the work of the speculative realists my philosophical heroes were the American pragmatists Charles Sanders Peirce and William James.[14] When I began my earnest study of pragmatism, what drew me to it was the boldness of inquiry that its founders embarked upon. I quickly realized that pragmatism was much more an attitude and method of inquiry than a set of philosophical ideas about reality. Now I recognize that the pragmatists' project might best be seen as an early formulation of speculative realism.

The motto of Charles Sanders Peirce was, "Never block the road to inquiry." By this he meant that we should always move intellectually in directions that open up more inquiry, not less. This is not the typical view of inquiry, because generally we think of truth as

---

[14] Pragmatism is America's greatest contribution to world philosophy. It is based on an assumption that the truth of any idea can only be found by acting on it and witnessing the difference it makes to believe in it. At its essence pragmatism is a form of inquiry, and in that sense I see speculative realism as an extension of the spirit of pragmatism.

something that we converge toward, not something we expand into. In other words, we begin our inquiry with many possibilities and eliminate them one by one until there is only one possibility left. At that point we have come to the truth, and our inquiry has come to an end.

Peirce and James were compelled by Darwin's conception of evolution by natural selection, and they realized that an evolving universe was fundamentally different from a static one and required a different form of inquiry. A static universe is finite and fixed and therefore knowable. In a static universe we find the truth among what already exists. An evolving universe is in a state of growth and flux. Because of this the truth of this moment won't necessarily hold until the next. We can never come to an end of inquiry because the universe we live in is growing. So Peirce and James advocated perpetual inquiry as the most appropriate philosophical stance to take in a universe that is growing.

This led both Peirce and James to the creation of wildly imaginative conceptions of reality that I will outline briefly here. I am not presenting them because they represent any definitive truth about reality. I offer them only as visions of reality that in many ways take us beyond dualistic, human-centered, things-in-space consciousness and bring us a little closer to a continuity-unfolding conception of reality. Their true value is that they can spur us into broader speculation about reality and liberate our imaginations. You will also see that these ideas can be engaged with in a way that offers yet another opportunity to practice the Art of Staying on the Inside and continue our dance at the edge of yet another wormhole that promises the chance of falling into an experience of Radical Inclusivity.

Peirce questioned the fundamental categories of reality that Kant asserted shape our experience. The Kantian categories include space, time, and causality, and together, so Kant proposed, they create a framework that definitively and inescapably molds our experience of reality. These categories exist prior to everything else. And if we are locked into a human-centered view we will assume that the universe evolved within this preexisting container of time, space, and causality. Peirce took exception to this notion. If time, space, and causality are part of the universe, they must also have evolved. This deceptively simple notion, obvious at first glance, has enormous implications, and it opened Peirce to wild speculations about the evolution of everything.

Were moments in time always ordered sequentially? This may seem like a weird question to ask, but remember weirdness is exactly what we must embrace if we are to wormhole our way into a new reality.

Maybe the first moments of time appeared in random order—one now; one in the year 2012; the next ten days in the past; another four months in the future; then one a thousand years in the past; and on and on. Eventually two moments appeared in sequential order and had the survival advantage of having twice as much time for things to happen in. Through the process of natural selection all of the nonsequential moments died out of existence leaving only sequential moments. We enter into a universe filled with only sequential moments and assume it must always have been that way. The same may be true with space; perhaps spots in space were not always adjacent. And again with causality, maybe things happened randomly initially, and causality only gradually developed. Peirce's radical inquiry gives us a glimpse of how much we take for granted that, if we aspire to enter into a new reality, we must learn to question.

Peirce was practicing the Art of Staying on the Inside in his contemplation of evolution. If we live in an evolving universe, then everything must evolve, not just animal species as Darwin had so brilliantly explained, but everything. All of reality as we experience it today must have come into its present form through the process of evolution. Evolution must include everything.

Peirce was aware of the limitations of human understanding. He was not antirealist, however, because he did believe in a reality beyond our human perception of it. In fact, he was driven to determine what the truly essential characteristics of an evolving universe were. Everything must be included in the process of evolution, and so nothing could have been here at the start of the process. Peirce's inquiry was about what features must have been the absolutely first to have appeared out of the original nothingness in order to initiate a process of evolution. His inquiry led him to identify two absolutely necessary initial conditions of reality.

The first was spontaneous creation, the possibility of novelty, the ability for things to occur purely by chance. Without spontaneous happenings, nothing new would ever emerge, and the universe could not evolve. Novelty alone was not enough, however, because a universe containing only the ability for novelty would result in a never-ending cascade of chaotic creativity. The stability of the universe also required a tendency toward habit. Once something occurs once it must be more likely to happen again. This tendency toward habit assures some degree of order in the universe.

An evolving universe requires only two initial conditions as a starting point: the ability to change and the tendency to stick. The universe is made entirely out of change that sticks.

Mind, matter, life, nonlife is all one flowing mass of being that, at its very bottom, has only two characteristics—spontaneous chance and the tendency to form habits. Reality is a surge of existence that pours out like liquid into time and space. And that liquid is not equally fluid everywhere. In some places it is thin and runs like water, passing quickly from one form to another. In other places it is viscous like oil or gelatin and oozes slowly from shape to shape, remaining fixed for a time before reforming. In still others the liquid runs more like glass, flowing so slowly that its movement can only be seen across vast expanses of time. Human beings do not hold a privileged place in this reality. We are simply another form of change that sticks just like everything else.

William James was Peirce's lifelong friend and colleague. Peirce complained that James' philosophy was overly human-centered, but I believe you will see that James in his way was also blazing a trail beyond human perspectives.

In his masterwork *The Principles of Psychology* James embarked on a magnificently bold exploration not only of psychology, but also of reality itself. One of the topics he covered was time. He realized that typically we think of time as occurring in discrete durations that we refer to as moments. We imagine that the stream of time unfolds moment after moment in an unending chain. We imagine that each moment is separate from the one that came before and the one that will come after it. One of the problems with this view is that we have to account for our memories of the past. If each moment is discrete and separate from the one just passed, how does any information about the past enter into the present moment?

Typically the way we solve this problem is by imagining the existence of a transcendent self, or ego, that is present during each moment of our lives and remembers events from past moments in the present. James was adamantly opposed to this form of duality. He would not accept the existence of a self that abides in a realm outside of time and space that holds our memories for us.

If there were no transcendent self that passes through moment to moment, then we can only account for memory by assuming that there are not hard boundaries separating one moment from the next. Each moment must blur into the next more like successive waves on the ocean than train cars on a track. James speculated that what we experience as the present moment is the height of intensity of a moment that trails off infinitely into the past. There can be no discrete place where one moment ends, and so each moment must extend infinitely. Our experience of this moment contains a great deal of the experience of the last moment along with it. It contains some, but less, of the moments from last week, and it has at least some trace of every moment that ever occurred. If every moment trails off infinitely in the past, that means that the trails of all future moments must be included in this one. Time is a continuum in which every moment includes every other moment. A great deal of the immediate past and future still exist in the present moment, but some speck of even the unimaginably distant past and future must also exist in the present.

As James continued on his own journey into Radical Inclusivity, he realized that everything must exist on the inside of a universe that contained no gaps. The universe was continuous in every way. There could be no slice or divide that completely separated any part of reality from any other. The conception of reality that James proposed to hold the fact of total continuity was a world made of pure experience.

For James the world was made up of pure experience in an additive process, with each new experience moving beyond and yet including the one before. He likened this to the way words form in our mouths and minds. When I read the word *dog* on a page, I may start out seeing the letters, but once the experience of each letter unfolds in awareness it leads to the formation of the concept of dog, which leapt out of the letters but contains much more. Metaphorically, this is how the universe unfolds. Successive experiences leap forward out of the last, adding a little more to reality. At the same time events of the future that have not been fully experienced yet exert an attractive force that calls the current experience forward.

James' brand of Radical Inclusivity was an inquiry into the fact that absolutely everything is made up of experience. The scene in front of me is an experience. The computer I am typing on is made up of my experiences of it. Even my body and mind are all made up of pure experience. No matter where you look for something that is not an experience, the moment you find it you will realize that you have only found another experience. Experience is the stuff that reality is made of.

The transcendent self is not a part of me that exists in some realm outside of experience. It is a fantasy that is created out of a succession of experiences. It appears to us that while we are aware of an object we are also aware of being aware of the object. In this way we experience ourselves as being self-conscious. There appears to be a "me" that is aware of the object and another "me" that is aware of the "me" that is aware of the object. These are not two different "me's." They are simply two different experiences in the ongoing flow of consciousness.

Self-awareness is not a separate vantage point from which I view myself. It is just another experience in the stream of consciousness. At one moment I am aware only of the object; in the next moment I am aware of myself; and then again I am aware of myself being aware of the object; and then only aware of the object again; and so on, one experience after another in a continuous flow. There is no transcendent self; there is only an experience of being aware of myself that periodically appears in the stream of consciousness.

The view of reality that James ignites in me is one of total continuity in a never-ending unfolding. Everything has a peak of intensity in time and space and spreads out from there infinitely in all directions.

Of course I cannot even describe this without falling into the unavoidable assumption of things-in-space consciousness. Too easily I fall into imagining everything as a thing that spreads out infinitely into three-dimensional space through two dimensions of time. That is the best my things-in-space mind can do. Luckily, I can do better because I already know that mind extends into the darkness beyond the cone of light created by the lamppost of the known. This is where the skillful application of Coleridge's suspension of disbelief comes into play.

We cannot get to a new reality by reaching out and puling it into our current reality. It won't fit in there. Like Dorothy clicking her heals to return home from Oz, we have to find a way to close our eyes and open them in the recognition that we were there all along. Our minds already exist in the new reality; we are simply not looking at that part of our mind yet.

My things-in-space mind is not going to understand the new reality. It will always take any experience of Radical Inclusivity and smash it back into the box of dualistic thinking, but I can do better. I can ignore my mind's sensibilities and throw out all notions of time and space. I can enter directly into my current experience of this moment and see that there is no time or space here—there is only the experience of time and space. This experience of reality that I am having has no dimensionality to it. It has not height, width, or thickness. Any sense of dimensionality or time is itself only an experience. Even the sense that I am having an experience is an experience. There is no one having this experience; there is just an experience of being someone having an experience. This experience of the present moment is all there is. It is unbroken, continuous, and whole, and it seems to be unfolding and expanding, or at least it contains an experience of expanding and unfolding.

Everything is inside of experience. The present moment contains all that there is. As we explore more and more deeply the implications of this radical view, we find ourselves moving far outside the confines of the holodeck or the lamppost. We cannot wrap our minds around an all-inclusive present moment in which everything is recognized as already being only another experience. If we keep practicing the Art of Staying on the Inside in this inquiry, we will find ourselves over and over again falling back into some things-in-space variation of a world bound by three-dimensions of space and two-dimensions of time. As many times as we fall into it, we can break out of it. Just like in meditation, we have to keep breaking out of the things-in-space habit of believing that we could be doing something other than allowing things to be as they are.

Our success demands that we embrace the wildly imaginative posture of the Romantics, the pragmatists, and the speculative realists. We must learn to hold our conceptions of reality loosely, squeezing no harder than you would hold an open tube of toothpaste. We have to learn to use language in ways that move us forward without ever tying us down. Our words and conceptions need to become tricky and devious, especially to ourselves. They need to coax us forward with prods and promises that never say enough to satisfy. We should stop to ponder only lightly before moving on to the next. If we aspire to fall through a wormhole that leads to a new reality, we must keep the dance moving to increase our likelihood of falling over the edge.

We must learn to question everything over and over again. Our minds are so constrained by our current conception of reality, but *we* do not have to be. The miracle of Radical Inclusivity is the recognition that we already exist beyond where our minds can go. There is nowhere to go because I am already there. If reality is truly continuous, then there is nowhere that I am not already because there could never be a hard line that separated me from everything else. I am not bound by my body or my mind. The edge of my skin is not the end of my being. The limits of my understanding are not the limits of my consciousness.

This sounds like nonsense to our things-in-space mind because that consciousness only trusts what it can stand apart from and look back at. Finding ourselves embedded in a mysterious and often brutal world, we learned to separate ourselves, to stand apart from the world and look back at it from a detached position so that we could study, understand, and ultimately control it. This process of objectification was developed culturally during the Enlightenment, and we are all masters of it. In fact, our habit of objectification is so strong and all pervasive that it has created a deep split in our experience of ourselves.

We are addicted to self-awareness.

Things-in-space consciousness validates reality through the process of objectification. It only trusts what it can turn toward and look at as an object separate from itself. It does not trust things that it cannot see. We even begin to doubt our own existence if we cannot see ourselves. If you consciously attempt to stop looking back at yourself, you will find a tremendous anxiety growing inside you; at least I did.

I remember an experience in meditation where I stopped being able to see myself. A tremendous fear built up. I was sitting on a chair, and my body began to shake with terror. It was as if I were dying. Suddenly a thought crossed my mind reminding me that there was no way I was going to die sitting on that chair. I relaxed and was astonished to find myself falling completely out of my mind and out through the back of my head. It was as if I had been living in a swirl of thought and feeling for my entire life, and now I was free-floating in a sea of pure awareness. I could no longer see myself. I had no body, no mind . . . nothing. I was not there anymore, and yet awareness continued.

One of the obstacles to a new consciousness is our need to see ourselves in it. To become vulnerable to the possibility of dramatic shifts in consciousness we have to give up the need to see ourselves there, because the consciousness we have now cannot see into the next. The consciousness of continuity unfolding must reintegrate that split. So our journey into this new consciousness necessitates that we face the challenge of letting go of a part of ourselves that feels like an indispensable validation of our existence.

Things-in-space consciousness with its need for validation from an external source demands that we always exist, at least in part, on the outside looking in. This is exactly the position that Radical Inclusivity forces us to relinquish. We surrender our right to remain outside and then recognize that the act of stepping outside was always already on the inside. There is no outside to life. Life is a playing field that has no sidelines. There is no boundary that we can step across that takes us out of the game. Any time we step across a boundary, that becomes part of the game.

Surprise, you're already here!

There is no outside and no separation, and there never has been. When we slip through a wormhole and find ourselves in continuity unfolding, we won't find ourselves someplace new; we will simply discover that we were here all along. We didn't go anywhere because there is nowhere to go.

I am here writing this book. You are there somewhere, a few hours, days, weeks, months, or years from now, reading it. The fact that we are not together is obvious and indisputable. Or is it?

Am I not there with you wherever you are? Are you not experiencing me through these words? Are you not here with me as I write with you in mind even if we have never met in the physical sense?

We have a habit of relentlessly locating ourselves in the experience of the embodied present. Here where I feel my fingers touching this keypad and see the words appearing on the screen in front of me is where I locate myself. I feel like I am "here" and not "there" with you as you read these words. You, on the other hand, feel that you are where your eyes are coming into contact with the print on the page or screen. You tie your existence to the circumstance where you are reading these words.

I experience myself to be the one who is typing; you experience yourself to be the one who is reading. The fact that we are separate is obvious and indisputable.

The fundamental separation that we feel in time

and space with other people is something we need to challenge. Is it true? Am I limited to this body and mind? Is it possible that I extend beyond it? And if I do, are there any limits to what I am, where I am, or when I am? Find the limits. Find the place where I end and you begin and nothing crosses over. If there were such a place, how could we connect at all?

The experience of being an embodied mind is an important part of who we are, but it is not the limit of who we are, or even the essence of who we are.

Maybe we exist everywhere we have an effect. Maybe there is no place where we do not have an effect. Perhaps I am there with you while you read this book, even though you are not reading it under the same circumstances of time and space that I am writing it.

I believe that our current experience of being human is just the beginning. If we are willing to suspend our disbelief long enough, we will discover possibilities for human existence that we cannot imagine. Maybe if I suspend disbelief long enough I can experience myself with you right now as you read this book sometime in the future from where I sit writing it.

AFTERWARD

This book was meant to be a dance along the edge of a wormhole. Hopefully you fell in, at least a little. Nothing I wrote here was meant to be definitive; it was all meant to invite you to a profound level of inquiry.

My whole point can be summed up by saying that reality is very different from our experience of it, but nevertheless we are in direct contact with it and always have been. By practicing the Art of Staying on the Inside and daring to expand our minds into the unimaginable we can gain access to a reality that we are already in contact with even when we don't realize it.

If I have been able to convey even a small recognition of this miraculous possibility, then my time spent in writing is well rewarded.

Jeff Carreira

ABOUT THE AUTHOR

Jeff Carreira originally received an undergraduate degree in physics and spent five years working as a research engineer before realizing that life's deepest questions could not be answered through science alone. He decided to work in a more humanitarian field and received a master's degree in education and spent seven years working as a special-education teacher and school administrator.

He embarked on a life devoted to awakening in 1992 when he met spiritual teacher Andrew Cohen and embraced the perspective of Evolutionary Enlightenment. A series of life-changing experiences led him to become a prominent member of a global spiritual movement where he created educational programs that supported the ongoing spiritual growth of thousands of people around the world.

Currently he works with Patricia Albere co-leading the Evolutionary Collective. In their collaborative work they explore the transformative possibilities of a higher order of human relatedness. Together they support the growth and development of an international community of people who are committed to living on the emerging edge of Spirit's unfolding.

Jeff is passionate about philosophy because he is passionate about the power of ideas to shape how we see ourselves and how we live. His enthusiasm for learning is infectious, and he enjoys addressing student groups and inspiring them to develop their own powers of inquiry.

In a world in which university education is often thought of as a vocational certificate, seeing someone obviously relishing the acquisition and sharing of knowledge for its own sake is inspiring.

—Dr. William O. Shropshire

Jeff has taught university students about Charles Darwin's influence on American thought, spoken with recovering alcoholics about the transformative philosophy of William James, and addressed Unitarian church groups about Ralph Waldo Emerson and the roots of their faith. He has taught college courses on philosophy, spoken at conferences, and led seminars worldwide.

He is the author of two books, *The Miracle of Meditation* and *Philosophy Is Not a Luxury*, and the co-author with Patricia Albere of a third book called *Mutual Awakening*.

For more information about Jeff or to book him for a speaking engagement, visit:

www.philosophyisnotaluxury.com

Made in the USA
Middletown, DE
06 May 2015